THREE ESSAYS

TAHIR SHAH

THREE ESSAYS

TAHIR SHAH

MMXXII

Secretum Mundi Publishing Ltd
Kemp House
City Road
London
EC1V 2NX
United Kingdom

www.secretum-mundi.com
info@secretum-mundi.com

First published by Secretum Mundi Publishing Ltd, 2022
VERSION 12102021

THREE ESSAYS

© TAHIR SHAH

Visit the author's website at:
Tahirshah.com

ISBN 978-1-912383-94-8

CONTENTS

CANNIBALISM:
IT'S JUST MEAT...?

THE PROTAGONIST OF a novel I once wrote is a surgeon who develops a secret delight in eating human eyes.

The more of them he devours, the more he begins to realize that human flesh — and eyes in particular — are a kind of manna sent from heaven. And what's more, he comes to understand that, when eaten, eye tissue has an astonishing and ameliorating effect on the human psyche. He doesn't understand why we're not all scoffing down our friends and neighbours — as research suggests our ancient ancestors probably did.

Last night, while sitting in bed, I read my wife a random passage from the work, which is called *Eye Spy*. The main character had just sucked out a drug addict's eyes in Paris. Clasping hands to her cheeks, my wife let out a shrill scream and then exclaimed:

'You can't publish that!'

'Why not?'

'Because people will be horrified.'

'Who will?'

'Everyone will,' she said.

Cannibalism has been described as the last taboo, and is the one that seems to shock the masses more than anything else. It's right up there with incest, cold-blooded murder, and human sacrifice. In researching my novel, I have done a great deal of background reading on the subject, and have found myself wondering constantly why we regard it with such disdain — after all, dead people are just meat, aren't they?

I think the answer lies in the way our society has structured itself around great monolithic pillars of right and wrong. An advanced culture has to lay down certain ground rules, without which a kind of disintegration begins to occur or, rather, without which advancement can't take place. It may seem like obvious stuff, but I'd argue that it isn't obvious at all.

As I see it, thinking that cannibalism is wrong is a hugely sophisticated idea, one that took millennia to become ingrained in human civilization. After all, most animals are quite happy to eat their own kind. I found a list of almost two thousand species online that regularly gulp down their mates, their young, or those around them. With the exception of apes perhaps, the animal kingdom doesn't have anything the majority of us would regard as real civilization. And so, I suppose we can draw a baseline under our society and say, 'We are civilized because we don't eat people.'

The same can't be said for a great many of the generations which came before us. There's no doubt at all that ancient man ate his fellow men in a great many places and circumstances.

I'll come to that in a moment.

All the more interesting is that cannibalism was, it seems, a tolerated taboo across almost all societies until relatively recent times. It's a subject that is nailed to the bedrock of our world, infused within our cultures through folklore and religion. There are plentiful examples of blood-gorging cannibalistic deities, for instance, whose actions provide cautionary tales for mankind.

The Greek myths are an entertainment often poised on the edge of acceptability, as much as they are a body of folklore. Their shock value makes them compulsive reading. But however depraved the taboo-shattering tales are, the Classical myths are always tempered with a kind of righteousness. The bad guy (or I should say, the bad deity) usually comes a cropper on the grand scale of things, and he's taught a lesson that's passed down to us all.

The Greek god Kronos was an example of a deity seemingly unfazed by the thought of eating his fellow kind. Fearful that his own children would usurp him, he gobbled up five of them in a row. Kronos was married to his own sister (itself an example of incest being rather less taboo than cannibalism), and she conspired to hide their sixth child — Zeus — in fear that he would be gobbled up, too.

In his wisdom, the young deity fed his father an emetic, which caused him to regurgitate Zeus's siblings. Happily, and rather amazingly, they all survived unharmed.

Another strange cannibalistic tale from the Greek myths concerns Pelops. He was killed and stewed up by his father, Tantalus, who fed the meat to the gods in an elaborate banquet. Having caught on to what was set before them, the deities didn't touch the meal, none except for Demeter who ate part of the boy's cooked shoulder. On Zeus's orders, the flesh and bones were boiled up once again and, the shoulder having been recreated from ivory, the boy was somehow cooked back into his original form. Tantalus (from whose name we get the word 'tantalize') was punished by being made to stand in a pool of pristine water, with the branches of a fruit tree hanging over him. Whenever he stooped down to drink, the water receded, and whenever he reached up for the fruit, the branches rose up into the air.

For all their rip-roaring action and intrigue, the Classics are in a realm of their own, one adrift on a sea of fantasy. They fall under the same umbrella as Hansel and Gretel (if you recall, the witch in the story ate little boys), and Sweeney Todd, the demon barber of Fleet Street. But the most memorable character among recent cannibalistic phenomena was undoubtedly Dr. Hannibal Lecter of *The Silence of the Lambs* fame.

Lecter sends shivers down our collective spines for the way he preys on the audience's raw fear, while operating with savvy and audacious method. The genius of the story is, of course, using a cannibal to catch a cannibal. This, coupled with the fact that Lecter was a connoisseur of high culture, made him a devastatingly irresistible anti-hero.

Coming back to reality, there's no shortage of evidence that our ancient ancestors ate each other. Archaeologists and anthropologists have pinpointed examples on a global scale of primitive humans feasting on their fellow men. Despite appreciating the attention they attract for suggesting cannibalism existed at sites uncovered at their digs, archaeologists usually have a hard time in deciding what kind of man-eating actually went on. Did our ancestors really chomp away at their dead on a daily basis, or was it a practice they indulged in only during famine and occasional bouts of warring?

The answer is probably more of the latter than the former. Even then, the main evidence is based on finding bones that have been scraped clean of their flesh with flint tools — such as the remains of Peking Man from 750,000 years ago, discovered outside modern Beijing.

In addition to eating the meat on a human carcass, it's certain judging from remains that ancient man delighted in extracting marrow from the long human leg bones. The delicacy would have provided a great source of protein. As for the question whether there were human communities that dined exclusively on their own flesh, it's very unlikely.

The reason is intriguing, and is to do with the weight of meat on a lean human frame. Our ancestors were hunters and so they weren't obese, but trimmed down to the point of continual hunger. Even then, a family group would have required several adults a week to satisfy their calorific needs. If they had lived exclusively on human meat, it would have led to the decimation of communities as large as their own within a very short time.

The thing that fascinates me though is the squeamishness with which we regard cannibalism in the modern Occidental world. This is totally at odds with attitudes throughout history in Europe and beyond. I would say that stories like Hansel and Gretel are part of an older culture, one in which cannibalism was an accepted way to behave.

During the Crusades, for example, it seems that people-eating was relatively widespread. This was certainly a result of starvation, but also a curious way of shaming the foe.

Eating the enemy was the ultimate act of humiliation. One delicacy that crops up during the Crusades is the 'curried hand of Saracen'. The hand muscles would have provided not only protein, but a good level of taste as well. Consuming an enemy's hand would have been a kind of Statement of Conquest as much as it was a ready meal.

During the Middle Ages, Europe was brought to its knees time and again by famine and plague. In such times of social and economic upheaval, devouring victims was a natural way to survive, but even so it seems to have been a diet of last resort.

My thinking that cannibalism wasn't nearly so frowned upon as it is today is borne out by the fact that many thousands of Egyptian mummies were sold as medicine between medieval and Victorian times. Preserved in bitumen, the mummies were powdered, then formulated into an entire pharmacopoeia all of their own. Eventually though, the bizarre treatment lost its shine because murdered Egyptian children and slaves were discovered to have been shipped westward having just been mummified.

The obsession with mummies' curative powers is one that preoccupied both West and East for centuries. Sceptics may question whether this is the real thing, but I'd say that eating preserved bodies in any form is as cannibalistic as anything else. And there's an example that I just can't get out of my head. It's known as 'mellification' and involves the preservation of a body — in honey.

The practice supposedly occurred during the Middle Ages in Arabia and, in its truest form, is quite remarkable. People were encouraged to donate their bodies while still alive so that others (I assume family members) could benefit from a rare elixir created from them.

The individual would be encouraged to eat nothing but honey. With nothing else entering their alimentary canal, it was said that their sweat and excrement were strangely honey-like, and that they died quite soon. When they were dead, the corpse was placed in a stone coffin, itself filled with honey. It was supposedly left for a century or more before being opened. Eventually, the coffin would be unsealed, its human contents now having turned into a kind of preserved confection. This would be broken up and sold by weight as a remedy for all manner of ills.

It was only with the Age of Exploration that Europe — cloistered away from the farthest reaches of the world in its own isolation — really began to experience the kind of cannibalism their own ancient ancestors must have known. All of a sudden, travellers searching for new realms to plunder came face to face with the grand taboos of human culture — human sacrifice and cannibalism among them.

Almost every so-called 'primitive' society seemed nonchalant about cannibalism. Native peoples just about everywhere were found to be feasting eagerly on human flesh. Indeed, it must have been more a question of who didn't eat people than who did. A great many of the European trailblazers themselves disappeared, devoured in distant climes by cheery tribesmen.

It's easy to imagine the titillation and the horror with which sailors' tales entertained European society. The more brutal and seemingly depraved, the more delight there must have been. It's likely that in many cases the cannibalistic stories were hammed up, but I think it's probable that a great many were recorded as they happened.

We get our word 'cannibal' from the Spanish name for the Carib people of the West Indies, who had a long and proud history of consuming enemies slain or captured in battle. This extended of course to early European adventurers, such as the Italian explorer Giovanni da Verrazzano. He was killed at Guadeloupe in the year 1528, and was eaten in a stew.

It's difficult to say how much of the legend relating to the Carib Indians is hysterical supposition, and how much is based on cold hard fact. My own thinking is that, however barbaric the Carib people might have been, they were hardly more ruthless than the Spanish Conquistadors who had arrived to slaughter them. Naturally, the Spanish filled many books with the misdeeds of the peoples they had encountered, while hardly making mention of their own extraordinary barbarities (such as feeding their victims with their own testicles).

What is certain is that on the American mainland — north and south — a great many cultures regarded cannibalism as an essential backbone of animistic culture. And, in sheer scale, their people-eating endeavours must have far exceeded anything going on over in the Caribbean.

At the time of Columbus, South America was awash with tribes engaging in people-eating. The practice appears to have been so widespread that it was almost ubiquitous.

My favourite reliable account of Latin American cannibalism was recorded in the pages of a sixteenth-century book written by Hans Staden, a German soldier and adventurer. He voyaged into Brazil in 1549, where he was shipwrecked and marched into the jungle by the Tupinamba Indians. The tribe planned to eat him, but kept him in a cage to fatten him up first. But when Staden cured their chief of illness, the tribe spared his life, albeit reluctantly.

After many trials and tribulations, Staden escaped, and made his way back to Europe, where his tale of the cannibalistic traditions of his former captors became an international bestseller of the time. During his long captivity, Staden was fed what he described as a 'delicious soup', served up in a cauldron. While helping himself to more, he realized there were human skulls at the bottom of the pot. He recognized the individuals he was eating from their cooked faces. They had been his friends.

To the north, in what's now Mexico, Aztec society was practising cannibalism on a grand scale as well as that other shameful taboo — human sacrifice. Their elaborate rituals entailed thousands of people being sacrificed each year, offerings that formed part of a strict devotional system. Historians have suggested that the Aztecs were in a constant state of war because of the sheer number of victims needed by their priesthood.

When Spanish Conquistador Hernando Cortés arrived in Mexico on his quest for gold, he was dismayed to find cages packed with people who were going to be slaughtered in the name of ritualistic food. He recorded first-hand accounts of them having their hearts cut out while still alive, and their bodies thrown to the populace — once the precious internal organs had been chopped out by the priests.

Recent excavations in Colorado have suggested that the Pueblo Indians engaged in cannibalism too, probably as part of ritualistic sacrifice — I imagine similar in nature to that of the Aztecs.

But the idea of North Americans — past or present — eating each other is a touchy subject. I can't quite understand why.

After all, it seems likely that more human societies through history have dabbled in cannibalism than have not. But we're still all appalled by the thought of it.

As the Age of Exploration pushed the boundaries of discovery ever farther, cannibals were discovered across the Pacific and in the distant reaches of the Antipodes. And with all the voyages, there were plenty of shipwrecks.

In such cases there was sometimes no choice but to draw straws and serve up one of the crew. This form of cannibalism — in the name of survival — is in a class of its own. I'd argue that in normal circumstances the shock-horror value would be rather minimal. But it was somehow amplified by the fact that those eaten, and those doing the eating, were usually ordinary people just like us. The question is always: 'In the same circumstances, what would you do?'

The most famous case of murder to provide meat for survivors came to court in 1884. It involved four survivors of an English yacht, the *Mignonette*, being stranded in a lifeboat 1,600 miles from the Cape of Good Hope. Having fallen unconscious, the cabin boy was killed by the others, who then ate part of his body. They were picked up a few days later, and two of the men were eventually found guilty of murder.

Another case that caused great shock more recently was the fate of the Uruguayan rugby team, whose small aircraft crashed in the Andes during the winter of 1972. Of the initial forty-five passengers and crew, only sixteen survived — and most of those only did so by consuming the meat cut from their dead friends. They cooked strips of it in the sun, then forced it down. The story based on Piers Paul Read's book, *Alive*, went on to become a Hollywood movie starring Ethan Hawke.

Inspired by Hans Staden's account, I have myself always been intrigued by the idea of how human meat would taste. An experience a few years ago introduced me, I think, to a flavour very similar, if not precisely the same.

I had travelled to the headwaters of the Upper Amazon in Peru, researching a book about the flora-based hallucinogen *ayahuasca*, and the tribe of the Shuar who take it. Until a century ago the Shuar were infamous for the way they would shrink the heads of their foes to about the size of a grapefruit, by crushing the skull and then reducing the envelope of skin with hot sand.

For many weeks I pushed upriver in a derelict boat that I had hired downstream in Iquitos. She was rather like the *African Queen*, and I was her wayward skipper, with a crew of degenerates. The most reprobate of all was a Vietnam vet who had promised to keep me alive in the jungle. He spent most of his time lying stoned on the deck.

From the moment we approached the Shuar's hunting grounds, the crew began trembling with fear. They had all heard the stories, the tales of the savage tribe who gorged themselves on intruders.

Night after night we feasted on giant capybara rodents and on tapir. Their meat was tough, very gamey, and was usually barbecued over termite nests. It was the only way to kill the worms.

Finally, early one evening, we reached a Shuar village. One of the tribesmen came down to the boat and brought an offering. In the half-light of dusk it looked curiously human.

It was a large roasted monkey.

The Vietnam vet, who lived in the Peruvian jungle (he could never bring himself to leave), ripped off the left arm and presented it to me.

'Eat it,' he said coldly, 'or the tribe will be unhappy.'

Not wanting to make anyone sad, I ate the whole thing — the biceps and the triceps, the meat of the forearm and the wrist. I remember my teeth reaching the hand. It was small and curled up, the fingers ending in prim little nails. There wasn't much flesh on it, not like the arm. As for the taste, it was delicious, succulent and strangely aromatic.

During my own travels in Africa, I have time and again struggled to pick up a trail that would bring me face to face with real-life cannibals. I was inspired by the late eighteenth-century explorer Mungo Park, who was in search of the distant kingdom of Timbuctoo. In his *Travels in the Interior Districts of Africa*, he described coming across slaves being prepared for shipment to plantations in the New World. Park noted that they were absolutely petrified because they believed they were destined for their captors' cooking pot.

The thought of cannibals dancing around a proverbial cauldron has fascinated me since childhood. In my late teens I was preoccupied with East Africa and used to visit Uganda during the civil war of the mid-1980s. Up in the so-called 'Luwero Triangle', I was shown far too many human skulls to count, each of them with a bullet hole in its rear. And I was told stories about Idi Amin, the former president, who was said by all to have indulged in plenty of cannibalism during his reign.

For decades I have tried to get to the bottom of the Idi Amin myth. I even wrote a book once for a man who was acquainted with him. The fee I negotiated was to have breakfast with the disgraced dictator in Saudi Arabia, where he was seeking refuge. Alas, though, the Last King of Scotland died of natural causes before we could share a meal together. It was a pity, because I had always wondered what he'd have served.

The reports of Idi Amin's years as leader make for gruesome reading. There's an account that at State House he kept the heads of his enemies in his fridges, and that he garnished the platters at a banquet with human body parts. My favourite is a quote that I understand is reliable. When asked if he ate human flesh, Amin retorted curtly, 'No, I don't like it. I find it too salty.'

At the same time that Amin was subjecting his countrymen to terror, Emperor Jean-Bédel Bokassa was doing the same, over in the Central African Republic.

Bokassa hit new heights on the 'deranged African dictator' scale. He thought he was a reincarnation of Napoleon Bonaparte — that is, Bonaparte with a cannibalistic edge.

By all accounts he had a taste for the tender meat of human babies, and would have them served up at dinners — satisfying his tastebuds, and horrifying his guests. When he was toppled in 1979, his freezers were supposedly found to be overflowing with gutted babies, their little bodies frozen hard as rock.

Whatever the truth of Amin or Bokassa, I am sure the cannibalism that would have appealed to them was a kind of shock-horror form — it certainly wasn't done as a solution to a shortage of food. My own experiences in the Dark Continent have borne out the idea of cannibalism as a kind of method of control, rather than as a source of nourishment. I have travelled in Ethiopia a great deal during famines, and have never once heard of a case of cannibalism there. Even though ordinary people were wasting away — dying in front of me — they didn't seem to be at all tempted by the thought of eating a fellow human's flesh.

But cannibalism certainly does continue in Africa today. Trawl the wire services and there are reports every so often, filtering through from local news sources. Almost without exception, they revolve around a kind of magico-spiritualism. It's all about expunging the memory of the deceased or, more importantly, about gaining something intangible from them — not protein, but power.

In the West African land of Sierra Leone, I once met a member of a fraternity who supposedly killed children and ate them. He was incarcerated in a small prison outside Freetown, having been caught with a human leg in his home. The jail was a ramshackle concrete hellhole, which stank of sewage and death. There must have been hundreds of men locked up there — charged with everything from petty theft to cannibalism.

The moment the gate was opened for me, I wished I had never had the bright idea of paying a visit. The prisoner I had come to see was called Milton and he had been sentenced to life. By the time I arrived, he had spent four years in solitary. There was such fear of him that he was permitted his own concrete box — in a jail where most of the inmates were crammed by the dozen into tiny cells.

Milton must have been in his fifties. He had unremarkable features, but a composure that instilled real fear into everyone around him. Even the jailer confessed he was terrified of him. When I asked if he had ever eaten human meat, Milton looked right through me. Then, very slowly, his mouth opened, and he said:

'And what is wrong with that?'

Call me old-fashioned, but the way I see it, it's surely far worse to actually kill someone than to eat them. But our society doesn't seem to agree with me. Every year there are so many homicides worldwide that only the grizzliest ones — or those involving celebrities — make a big splash. Yet any case involving cannibalism is instantly swept up by the press, with acres of column space devoted to it.

The *crème de la crème* of such a line in stories are those involving serial cannibals. That's where Hannibal Lecter fitted in. Real-life studies of cannibalistic serial killers are rare, needless to say, but they do crop up. And, oh, how the public devours them when they come along. Serial cases differ from other forms of cannibalism in that they're usually performed as a kind of psychotic perversion.

The most celebrated case in recent times was the American serial killer and all-round sex offender Jeffrey Dahmer. His other crimes involved homosexual necrophilia and a catalogue of other peculiar atrocities. Eventually found guilty of seventeen murders in the Milwaukee area, Dahmer was thought to have been murdering about one victim a week at his peak. It was only in the months after his apprehension that the true story of his orgy of death and cannibalism emerged.

Preying on gay men, he would pick out lonely individuals, invite them home for a beer, and have sex with them before killing them. At first he buried the bodies in the back yard, but, as he began to enjoy the process of killing all the more, there were too many bodies. And so, he changed tack.

He would photograph the naked corpses, have sex with them, then cut them open and sense the warmth emanating from them. Little by little he dismembered them, removing key organs or prime cuts of flesh, wrapping them in plastic, and freezing them. He boiled down the skulls and bleached them, before spray-painting them for his macabre collection. He chopped off the sexual organs, too, and pickled them in formaldehyde. The odds and ends of bone, sinew and meat were thrown in an oil drum filled with acid and reduced to an unctuous sludge that could be flushed away with the household sewage.

Jeffrey Dahmer shocked America, but fascinated it as well. After all, he was the real-life incarnation of Hannibal the Cannibal. As for Dahmer himself, he didn't manage to serve his fifteen life sentences. He was bludgeoned to death by a fellow inmate in November 1994.

In terms of pure weirdness, Dahmer has only been eclipsed by Armin Meiwes, a German from the small town of Rotenburg.

Meiwes placed an advert online on a site called the Cannibal Café. He said he was looking for 'a well-built 18- to 30-year-old to be slaughtered and then consumed'. A surprisingly large number of people contacted him, showing an interest in his request, before turning him down once they realized what he had in store for them. Meiwes selected a man named Bernd Jürgen Brandes and outlined his plan at their first meeting in March 2001.

Brandes agreed, and they repaired to Meiwes's little home in Rotenburg. The next thing Brandes knew was that his penis was cooking in garlic and a dash of wine on the stove. He had asked Meiwes to bite the organ off, a feat that proved too tricky, and so it was cut off with a knife. Brandes attempted to eat some of it himself but found it too tough and chewy.

Having videoed the ordeal, Meiwes went off to read a *Star Trek* book for some three hours, while his victim — plied with painkillers and schnapps — was left to bleed in the bath. Once Brandes was weakened by the tremendous blood loss, Meiwes killed him and began the process of dismemberment.

In the months that followed, he is said to have consumed about twenty kilos of Brandes's flesh, keeping specific organs and cuts in the freezer until he was ready for them. He had even planned to grind his bones into flour.

Towards the end of the following year Meiwes was arrested, having placed advertisements online in the hope of attracting another victim. His initial conviction of manslaughter was increased to murder, and he was sentenced to life imprisonment. While in prison, Meiwes has apparently repented his sins and become a vegetarian. He has even followed Hannibal Lecter's example and assisted German police in the analysis of two other suspected cannibal cases.

As for the protagonist in my novel, *Eye Spy*, the one that so horrified my wife, he shares Dahmer's and Meiwes's delight in eating people. I have heard it said that some firefighters find it hard to stomach bacon because it reminds them of the smell of roasting human flesh. I often turn that thought around in my head. You see, the monkey's arm I ate in the Amazon tasted of flame-grilled bacon. I sometimes wonder if my fascination for the subject would make me a good cannibal.

But I'm hoping that I'll never find out.

THE KUMBH MELA:
THE GREATEST SHOW
ON EARTH

THERE'S A BLUR of feet hurrying through ankle-deep mud.

Millions and millions of them. Some in plastic sandals, others in rubber boots, many others in cheap city shoes, or sneakers, or flip-flops, or brogues. Tens of thousands more are barefoot, some limping, others running.

This sea of humanity is surging forward, relentless and unstoppable. Most of them have bundles on their heads. Each one is stuffed with rice and flour, pots and pans, blankets and bedrolls. Many have babies bundled on their backs or toddlers clutched tight to their chests. Eyes squinting into the bright winter sunlight, they are streaming in from all points of the compass towards the vast encampment.

A sense of frantic anticipation and complete exhilaration unites them. As it does so, the unending torrent of pilgrims sets eyes on the glinting waters. It is the point where their journey ends just as it begins.

This is the greatest gathering in human history, a multitude of one hundred million souls. They've come to the Sangam, the confluence point where the subcontinent's two holiest rivers — the Ganges and the Yamuna — converge, at Prayag, outside Allahabad in northern India.

Once every 144 years a Maha Kumbh Mela takes place, Hinduism's vast ritualistic cleansing of souls. Translating as 'The Great Festival of the Urn', the last time it took place, Queen Victoria was on the British throne.

The India that usually makes the headlines is the one abundant with call centres and Rolls-Royce dealerships, and with skyscrapers that reach high above the landscapes of interminable urban sprawl. It's the India of Bollywood bling and of ubiquitous shopping malls, of ritzy brand names, and of the super-rich who can't get enough of all the über-kitsch.

Dedicated to wealth creation, this newfangled India of the twenty-first century defies logic just as it exceeds expectation. It may be a realm that makes the Occidental world drool with envy, but it's only a small fragment of what's really going on.

Travel through the Indian subcontinent and you quickly grasp that this is a land with its feet rooted firmly to the ground. The heads of the jet-set oligarchs may be in the clouds, but the majority of rank-and-file Indians have no doubt who they are, and where they've come from. Hailing from villages and small towns, the silent majority may aspire to gaining wealth too, but what's central to their lives is something that runs far deeper.

Faith.

And to most of them there's almost nothing in the ancient spiritual machinery of Mother India quite so auspicious as the Kumbh Mela. An immense cosmic counterbalance, an Indian Woodstock devoted to peace and love, it's the distilled essence of the subcontinent.

Pass a few days at the Mela's world within a world and you can't help but be sucked into it and swept along. As you learn to block out the ubiquitous hum of background noise, you begin to piece together the fragments that form the grand mosaic that is the Kumbh.

I first heard of it as a student backpacking around West Bengal twenty-five years ago. I was taking refuge from the monsoon under a railway bridge. Already sheltering there was a *sadhu*, who was travelling by foot. He was naked, covered in ash, with wizened limbs and an intense stare that has stuck in my mind ever since.

As the rain began to fall harder, he suddenly grabbed my arm.

'I will not get there in time!' he exclaimed anxiously.

'Get where?'

'To the Kumbh Mela!'

I asked him what it was.

'It is the union of the sky, the sun and the moon,' he said.

Unable to forget the holy man's words, I've often wondered if he did make it in time. Had he missed it, there would have been a lengthy wait for the next one, not to mention a long walk home to West Bengal.

Entangled in the astrological sequence of auspicious timings, the Kumbh Mela is held in one of four cities in strict rotation once every three years — at Nasik, Haridwar, Ujjain, and Prayag, where this year's festival was held. The locations of the Melas are said to be points at which droplets of Amrit, the Elixir of Immortality, were spilt in antiquity by the celestial Garuda bird.

Once every twelve years a great Kumbh Mela takes place, when the propitious timing is amplified many thousands of times over. And, in keeping with the lunar cycles, every twelfth great Kumbh Mela is the 'Maha' — held every 144 years.

Remembering the naked *sadhu* taking refuge with me under the railway bridge, and quite certain I wouldn't be here for the next one, I pledged to journey to Allahabad myself, to attend the Maha Kumbh Mela.

As someone well used to the grand scale of India, I assumed deep down that the festival would be nothing more than a whole lot of people whipped up into a spiritual frenzy. But the days and nights I spent there changed the way I view the subcontinent, and even the way I regard my fellow man. A primal human experience, it defied the complexities of contemporary life, while holding up a mirror to our collective souls.

Located a few miles away from Allahabad, most of the festival ground is more normally well underwater, beneath the sacred rivers. Organizers can never be quite sure how far the waters of the Ganges and the Yamuna are going to recede, and exactly which lands will be exposed.

Once the waters have retreated in late November, there's a wait before the ground has drained and hardened. Last year the waters receded much later than usual, which meant that the vast tent city could only be constructed at the last moment.

The festival ground has to be seen to be believed. With a hundred million people traipsing through during the fifty-five-day Mela, it's on a titanic scale. Covering almost five thousand acres, it's divided and sub-divided into numerous sectors on a grid structure.

One of the great difficulties is that the site straddles the intersection of the mighty Ganges and the Yamuna. This leads to a complicated natural arrangement of sandbanks and uneven connection points. To link them all together, dozens of pontoon bridges are erected, each of them buoyed by a series of massive iron drums.

On the surface, the tent city resembles something out of a military campaign. In addition to the pontoons and the neat rows of khaki tents, the main thoroughfares are laid with iron sheets so that vehicles don't get stuck in the mud. There's electric street-lighting too, which bathes the camp in an unnerving yellow glow through the hours of darkness. The lights are run by a series of mobile power stations, set up just for the Kumbh Mela.

But all this is just the tip of the logistical iceberg.

Dozens of police stations pepper the encampment, as do mobile field hospitals, fire stations and government offices. After all, in India, the wheels of bureaucracy die hard. And there are cafés, shrines, and trinket stalls by the thousand, as well as bandstands and rickety-looking fairground rides, and more than 35,000 portable loos.

Spend some time at the Maha Kumbh Mela and you quickly grasp that it's not about mind-numbing statistics. It's about people, and about their utter belief in a system of devotion that forms an unwavering backbone to life from the cradle to the crematorium.

For those of us raised in the cynical nihilism of the West, it may be hard to understand how or why a family living in a village a thousand miles away from Allahabad would blow almost everything they have to bathe at this auspicious moment at the Sangam, the confluence. But, regarded through the eyes of the devout majority, it's an affirmation of unshakeable belief. And central to that belief is the steadfast faith in a system that promises redemption in exchange for devotion.

If the figures are correct, and one in twelve of the entire Indian population passed through the Kumbh this year, then it reflects what this astonishing mass act of piety means to Hindus. They hastened to Allahabad from every corner of India — from each city, town, village and hamlet. They came from the tea plantations of Assam in the extreme north-east and from the desiccated deserts of Rajasthan, from the mountain stronghold of the Himalayas, and from the tranquil waterways of Kerala. They ventured, too, from the smog-filled urban sprawls of Delhi, Bangalore and Mumbai. They came to be united all together but, more importantly, they came to be absolved of their sins.

I reached the Kumbh Mela at dusk on Valentine's Day. Having taken a flight to Varanasi and then driven through the lush countryside for several hours, I knew we were nearing because of a rumbling sound on the wind. We must have still been ten miles out of Allahabad, but I could feel the Kumbh in my bones.

Asking the driver to stop, I got out and listened.

What I heard was like one of those nature films where they stick a microphone into a colony of ants. A cross between frenzied movement and what sounded like every conversation in the world overlaid on top of each other, it filled me with a primeval sense of fear as well as curiosity.

We continued and, as we did so, we began to pass droves of people on foot. Most of them were laden with belongings piled on their heads. Processing forward through wind and light rain they marched with an extraordinary surety of movement. It was as if the Maha Kumbh Mela was somehow in their DNA, that to get there was programmed into them all — whatever the cost may have been.

When in India, foreigners have a way of asking questions for which there are no black-and-white answers. As soon as I arrived, I begged everyone I met to give me facts and figures, and to tell me when the Kumbh Mela began. No one seemed sure. One man told me, 'It started ten million years ago.' Another was less exact. He said: 'It's been going a long, long time, sir.'

The first known foreigner to have written his impressions was the seventh-century Chinese monk Xuanzang (although some scholars have doubted whether he actually saw the Kumbh).

The earliest known account in English was written by the celebrated American traveller and novelist, Mark Twain. He described his visit to the festival of 1894 in *Following the Equator*. Of it, he said: 'It is wonderful, the power of a faith like that, that can make multitudes upon multitudes of the old and weak and the young and frail enter without hesitation or complaint on such incredible journeys and endure the resultant miseries without repining.'

I found myself wondering where Twain would have stayed on his visit more than a century ago. Fortunately for me, I was taken in at the lavish Laxmi Kutir camp, in a prominent position above the main festival site. It was situated between a Hindu temple and a Muslim mosque — both of which strove to outdo the other in terms of noise and commotion through day and night.

The camp boasted tents with ensuite bathrooms, feather quilts, and hot water bottles. There were even chocolates on the pillows at night. Having settled in, I went over to the viewing terrace, and got my first real glimpse of the Kumbh.

Glowing canary-yellow from all the thousands of improvised streetlamps, it was like nothing I had ever imagined. In the struggle to describe the spectacle it seems that only clichés are sufficient. It was like staring through a kaleidoscopic lens into the navel of the world, into a realm that defied both time and space. Humming, murmuring, and with whispers on the breeze, it was electrifying, empowering, and was more radiant in its sheer energy than anything I had ever seen.

After a couple of hours of trying to sleep in my prim tent, I got up. The vibrations from the plateau were calling me to come and join the fun. There was a sense of the Pied Piper about it, something so mesmerizing that I was quite unable to resist.

Clambering down steep steps cut into the rock, I climbed down to where tens of millions of ordinary Indians were camped. It was three a.m. but there were people everywhere. Some were washing or praying, many more were walking alone or with children in arms, all heading in the same direction — down to the Sangam.

Making my way through the unending landscape of tents, my eyes grew accustomed to the creamy yellow light. As for my ears, they were bombarded by the high-pitched chants from a thousand makeshift shrines. And mounted on poles every hundred yards were loudspeakers through which came continuous appeals of family members separated from their clans.

Following the hordes through the mud, I stumbled forward in mist tinged with yellow light over a series of pontoon bridges, down to the confluence. It was bizarre to think that for most of the year the land on which my feet were walking was the sacred riverbed. For the millions of pilgrims this was holy ground, the reason why a great many went barefoot.

The thing that sticks in your mind from the first moment is the sense of goodwill. In the days I spent at the Kumbh Mela, I saw too many spontaneous acts of kindness to recall: a pilgrim pressing a folded bill into a blind beggar's hand; a woman taking off her shoes and giving them to another who had lost hers in the mayhem; a little boy presenting his banana-leaf bowl of rice to a crippled old man on a cart.

Traversing a kind of beach, I finally got down to the actual waterline. Reinforced with sandbags, there was a flimsy wooden stockade screening the area off from a much larger expanse. On the other side of it there were literally millions of people surging into the water. Stripping off their outer garments, they were mesmerized by the auspiciousness of the moment.

The Mela began on 14th January at the Makar Sankranti, when the sun entered Capricorn, the day on which it's said that light returns after its long southward journey. A winter solstice, it signals the start of fifty-five days of providence. And during this festival time there are a series of extra-specially auspicious days. Believing their prayers will be amplified, pilgrims make sure they bathe at the Sangam then.

The day after my arrival was the second-most favourable of all, the reason why so many had got down to the water early — keen to beat the rush. With an ocean of people stretching as far as the eye could see, there was the constant fear of stampede. Kumbh Melas are notorious for masses of innocent people being trampled underfoot. All it takes is for one person to freak out and to run. There is in us all a primal fear of crowds, and it's triggered at such moments.

Like everyone else, I was tanked up with pure adrenalin, ready for fight or flight, and for the stampede. Unlike the pilgrims, however, my purpose was not to enter the freezing waters of the confluence, but to watch.

As I stood there on the less crowded side of the stockade, a policeman on horseback hurtled down the beach. Wielding a *latti*, a long wooden stave, he herded me and others into the narrowest pinprick of land between the water, the stockade, and the countless ordinary folk on the other side.

All of a sudden I made out the muffled cries of what sounded like an army roaring into battle. Turning quickly, squinting through the yellowed light, I saw a sight of true terror, like something from Hollywood's wildest fantasy.

Hundreds of naked men were making a beeline for
the spot on which I was standing. Their bodies caked in
ash, their hair matted in long twisted dreadlocks, some
were waving swords, others tridents or shields. More still
were chanting or howling, faces contorted with macabre
expressions, feet running in a crazed blur of movement.

Wave upon wave of them charged into the chill water,
immersing themselves, before retreating hastily onto the
beach. These *naga*s, holy men, are the revered mainstay of a
tradition dedicated to prayer, solitude, and to relinquishing
the trappings of conventional life. Their brotherhood, the
Order of the Juna Akhara, meaning 'Ancient Circle', is a
secretive monastic order of *sadhu*s, yogis and ascetics.

Such is their reputation for spiritual leadership, they
are given VIP pride of place at the Kumbh Mela. When
not bathing down at the waterline, they spend their days
smoking pipes stuffed with hashish in a special area reserved
just for them.

Dedicated to receiving *moksha*, liberation from continual
reincarnation, *sadhu*s (which simply means 'good men'),
crisscross the subcontinent most usually on foot, living
lives of stark austerity. They are sworn to celibacy and
shun material chattels, and spend a great deal of time
crouched beside a smouldering sacred fire known as a
dhuni. Rubbing the ash onto their naked skin, they pass the
hours smoking, meditating, and receiving the veneration of
ordinary people.

In the lanes of this VIP area, I came across all manner
of *avatar*s and holy men. A few were practising acts of

penance, their bodies contorted in strange positions, or their arms having been raised up in the air for decades.

It was there that I found Baba Rampuri.

Bespectacled, with sapphire eyes and with a great bush of teaselled greying beard, he was seated on a low dais. Uncharacteristically clean for a *sadhu*, he had hair that fell in curls to his shoulders; his clothing was spotless too: a loose saffron shirt and pyjama-style trousers.

Baba Rampuri said he had been coming to Kumbh Melas since 1971, the year in which he moved to India from the United States. A throwback to the age of tie-dye and navel-contemplation, he oozed peace, love, and goodwill to all men.

We spent the afternoon together, and in that time Baba Rampuri lifted the veil into the world of the ordained *sadhu*. A mystical fraternity with roots in India's ancient past, it's a society that sits awkwardly with the feverish consumerism that clouds any experience of modern urban India.

Leaning back on his dais, Baba Rampuri looked as though he'd seen it all before — a writer crouching before him eager for a usable soundbite. Then he told me that he had read some of the books I'd written and I punched the air in my mind. His hands churning around him, he said:

'No writer or photographer who's ever come to the Kumbh Mela has ever had a financial or artistic success. None of them. Not a single one.'

I asked why.

Rampuri grinned, albeit a sarcastic grin, one that made me shift my crossed legs uneasily.

'Because,' he said, 'you all tell it like it is, blinkered by the overwhelming seductive imagery. But you never tell the story behind the story. Here at the Kumbh there are a couple of worlds present at the same time. There's the one that's on the surface that intoxicates you, and the other that you hold in your heart.'

Baba Rampuri wagged a finger hard in my direction. 'It's not about me,' he said, 'but about the order of which I'm a small part. This institution has the ability to pass learning down through the time. I've devoted my life to the Ancient Circle of the Juna Akhara. And in that time I've seen that most foreigners miss the point. You all go on about how a pilgrimage like this is about nurturing the self. Well, it's not about the self but the group experience!'

During our conversations, Baba Rampuri would take the *chilam*, a clay pipe, from a fellow American guru, wrap a handkerchief over the end to filter it, and draw hard. His sapphire eyes clouding over, he railed against the foreigners who came to the Kumbh Mela and missed it all because they were too busy peering through camera lenses, and as a result failed to see what was going on.

All of a sudden the American *sadhu* waved a finger in my direction.

'We have to go and feed people now,' he said.

'Who?'

'Ordinary people.'

'How many ordinary people?'

Baba Rampuri pushed his rimless glasses up higher on his nose.

'About five thousand,' he said.

When I asked how he could afford it, the guru seemed a little despondent.

'Every member of the Juna Akhara leaves the Mela penniless,' he told me. 'We always do. It costs us way more than a hundred thousand dollars. Such great social responsibilities go along with it — of which feeding the masses is just one.'

Before I took my leave of Baba Rampuri, he told me to check out his website and to follow him on Facebook. I did a double take.

'You're in cyberspace?'

Reaching for the *chilam*, the American grinned one last time.

'Of course I am,' he said.

Leaving Rampuri to feed a small fraction of the entire pilgrim population, I strolled through the makeshift lanes of the Juna Akhara. Taking in the dozens of holy men, some naked and others not, I felt as though I had reached the innermost layer of onion skin. This seemed to be the spiritual core of an entire religious system, in a land with many hundreds of millions of followers.

I got talking to a Gujarati couple from Ahmedabad who had been prostrating themselves before an elderly *sadhu* — one who had supposedly taken a vow of silence back in 1962. The husband, Rajiv, told me that he worked ten hours a day in a call centre, and that he had brought his entire family to the Kumbh Mela to help balance the malevolent forces in the universe.

I asked what the naked *naga* would be able to do for them.

Rajiv touched a hand to his heart.

'He has given us his love and his blessing,' he said.

'But why do you feel you need it?' I asked cynically.

Rajiv's wife, Mahdvi, broke in.

'Because, it's the counterbalance for the world that we all live in.'

'And how is it — your world?'

Mahdvi shook her head glumly.

'It's a place of deadlines, stress, pollution, and without enough space — a place where you're suspicious of strangers and where you forget to see the beauty.'

'Which beauty?'

Rajiv held out his hands.

'The beauty that's all around us,' he said.

Back up at the deluxe Laxmi Kutir camp, I took a hot shower, scoffed down a four-course dinner, and felt rather ashamed of myself for feeling the need to regroup in the lap of luxury. At the next table I met an Englishman called Ronnie who had come to the Kumbh to look for an old school pal. A big, blustering bear of a man with broken veins speckled over his cheeks, he told me that he had been at Eton with Sir James Mallinson.

'He's down there somewhere,' said Ronnie distantly. 'Although I haven't a clue where to start looking. He's gone native, you see.'

I asked Ronnie what he meant.

'Well, after Oxford, Jim became a *sadhu*, and he was given the name Jadish Das. He's devoted his life to purifying himself.'

I asked Ronnie what his friend was like.

A little overcome with excitement, he exclaimed:
'Jim's a terrific chap — a real chum!'

For all its colour and curious traditions, the brotherhood of the Juna Akhara impressed me for the way it had remained on the rails. It may have been a beacon for eccentric Englishmen and for Californian ex-hippies, but there was something honourable about it. Most of all, I found myself appreciating what it hadn't become — a big-business Disneyland of the Soul.

The same couldn't be said for the dozens of godmen and godwomen who had set up temporary ashrams all over the Kumbh Mela. As the days passed, I couldn't help but become preoccupied by the sleek, well-oiled machinery of their high-flying guru businesses.

One afternoon I was making the long walk across the pontoons to the Sangam, when it began pouring with rain. Seeking shelter, I slipped into a giant canvas marquee in which a *darshan*, a meeting with a holy person, was taking place. Against the rhythmic drone of a tanpura, a woman dressed in a red turban was dispensing blessings to one and all.

Strangely, most of the followers were white Anglo-Saxon foreigners. Dressed identically in costumes of unblemished white, some had shaven heads, except for a Hare Krishna-style pigtail dangling from the back of the scalp. But they were not Hare Krishnas. They were instead zealous devotees of the Mauritius-born godwoman, Her Holiness Sai Maa.

Having jetted in for the Kumbh Mela from the community's Temple of Consciousness Ashram, just south of Denver, most of them were American, with other followers hailing from Germany, France, and Spain. Unified by their enthusiasm for neatly packaged mysticism, and by their blinding smiles, the devotees of Sai Maa stuck out a mile, as did the fraternity's organization.

Awash with press packs, plush white vehicles and printed schedules, with merchandising, photo ops and presence on social media sites, the godwoman's setup had to be appreciated for its slickness.

Having whispered that I was a journalist, I was instantly ushered past an office packed with computers and technicians, and welcomed into a pristine audience room decorated with bunches of plastic flowers. It was explained that Sai Maa took a vow of silence for four hours in the middle of each day, but that she was willing to break her vow and speak just to me.

Grunting thanks for the honour, I waited.

From time to time a blue-eyed devotee would shuffle in and out, blinding me with a smile. After I'd waited a little more, there was suddenly a sense of heightened anticipation, as though a VIP — or rather a god — was about to arrive.

A small door opened and the lady in the red turban wafted through.

I have met plenty of self-appointed godmen and godwomen in India before, but Sai Maa was different from all the rest. There was a sense that, despite the abundant trappings of the guru business, she was merely putting on a show. And the show was perfectly configured to be lapped up by the legions of Occidental devotees who were craving a figure such as herself.

All Sai Maa was doing was filling a niche.

Though struggling to speak at first, Her Holiness quickly found her voice. It was soft and mellifluous, gliding out through lips anointed in fuchsia-coloured gloss. During my audience, I learned that Sai Maa had moved from Mauritius to France at twenty-one, that she had sat on the City Council of Bordeaux, and that she still owned a chateau there. I learned, too, that she had two grown-up children. She had been quite late in becoming a self-styled god.

It became clear that there were big plans afoot in the Maa's Temple of Consciousness movement. Construction was at that very moment taking place downriver on the banks of the Ganges at Varanasi, to build an ashram in the shape of two intersecting hearts. Dedicated to Global Enlightenment, Sai Maa's work was already reaching a worldwide following through cyberspace.

In the middle of my audience, a stream of American devotees filed in. With shaved heads bowed low, they prostrated themselves before their deity. Having kissed her feet, some of them snapped pictures with their phones. Almost as soon as they had come, the disciples were ushered out by an officious blue-eyed henchman from LA. I felt like congratulating him because he had understood the crux of the guru business — the art of limiting access.

Once the white-clad devotees were gone, Sai Maa babbled away in florid soundbites for a long while. I wondered how to break free and claw my way back to the glorious human stew of the Kumbh Mela a stone's throw away outside. My break came when the godwoman's BlackBerry began to buzz. Squinting at the display, Sai Maa took the call, chattering away in French.

Fifty yards from where the godwoman was sitting with scrubbed-clean devotees waiting at the door, a wizened old woman from Bihar was lying on the ground. She was weeping hysterically, her ragged clothing all covered in mud.

'I lost my son in the crowd,' she sobs, 'and I don't know how I will ever find him again.'

As I watched, a stall-keeper selling fried orange *jalebis* strode up and helped her from the ground. He pointed up to a loudspeaker that was blaring a distraught appeal.

'You're not the only one lost,' he said tenderly. 'I'll take you to the place where you can speak on this thing, and it will find you your son.' He handed her a bowl of hot *jalebis* and together they set off towards the setting sun.

The next morning I was taken to the scene of a fire. Faulty wiring had short-circuited, setting a Jeep alight, the petrol tank of which had exploded. Miraculously, only two people had been killed. The smouldering remains of dozens of tents and charred belongings had been heaped up in a great pile. Helped by his sons, a slightly built man was picking through it all, his expression forlorn.

'We came all the way from Tamil Nadu,' he said, 'and we have lost everything we brought with us.'

I asked the man about his life. Like most of the people at the Kumbh Mela, he was from India's rock-solid underbelly.

'We are farmers,' he said, 'and we have a little land outside Chennai. We grow rice and have some buffalo as well. We have come here as an act of devotion, a devotion to the river. Of course we hope to be blessed in return, but the reason we are here is to give ourselves to the river.'

All of a sudden the sky darkened as though the end of the world had come. A sense of panic prevailed. Time was running out — before the deluge struck.

A young holy man wrapped in a saffron robe saw me standing in the makeshift street wondering what to do. Tugging at my wrist, he led me fast through the maze of uniform tents, as the wind whipped up once again. It was late morning but the sky was as dark as midnight. As the first raindrops gushed down, the young *sadhu* thrust me into his tent. His name was Hardwar, and his expression was so composed that I couldn't take my eyes off his face.

We sat in silence listening to the rain. Behind him was a cluster of *sadhu*s drawing quietly on their pipes. And beside him was a boy of fourteen with almond eyes and an orange turban wrapped tight around his head. Recently ordained into the order of the Juna Akhara, he was lying on his stomach playing a video game on his phone.

'We will be leaving soon,' said Hardwar, straining to make himself heard against the thunderous roar of rain, 'down to Varanasi, where we will camp at the crematorium ghat. Our prayers here are almost done.'

I asked what the Kumbh Mela meant to him. Hardwar's lips were touched with the faintest hint of a smile. 'It's a mirror,' he said, 'in which is reflected the heavens, the universe and the world.'

As the rain flooded down outside, turning the dust into ankle-deep mud, I told Hardwar about Sai Maa and her jet-set devotees. He thought for a moment, then tapped me on the knee.

'God descends to Earth and is always present at the Kumbh,' he said softly, 'but to find him you must search for the most unlikely person. In him or her is God.'

The downpour ended and I went back outside to wade through ankle-deep mud. As I struggled through it, I couldn't help thinking of the farmer from Tamil Nadu who had been a random victim of the fire. And my thoughts turned to the millions of farmers, like him, who rely on the Ganges for their lives.

I have heard it said that almost half a billion Indians depend on the waters of Mother Ganga for drinking water and for irrigating their crops. The subcontinent may be urbanizing quickly, but millions spend their lives toiling away on the patchwork of tiny ancestral farms which lie in the Ganges' path.

As a sacred waterway that is herself a goddess, Indians believe the Ganges cannot ever be defiled by the misdeeds of Man. She's above pollution. It's for this reason of course that people are quite happy to gulp down cups of her holy water, even though it's dark grey with silt and grime. Indeed, having bathed at the Sangam, a great many pilgrims filled little containers with the Ganges' hallowed water, to take home to family members and friends who were unable to make the journey to the Kumbh.

With such a colossal tide of humanity clustered on the same stretch of riverbank, local authorities have been increasingly worried about the environmental impact of the fifty-five-day event. Despite a mass of sandbags at the waterline, soil erosion has been considerable. But the real damage to India's goddess-river has been the pollution. Plastic bags may have been outlawed at the Kumbh Mela for the first time, but severe ecological damage was done if only by the mind-numbing amounts of raw sewage flowing into the sacred confluence.

After almost a week at the festival, I headed from my luxurious vantage point down to it one last time.

More people were arriving every moment.

Although I was exhausted from the crowds, the noise, the godmen and the wild hullabaloo, there was a sense of rebirth, as though the Kumbh Mela was reinventing itself for the newcomers.

I watched as an extended family stumbled down to the waterline, clutching a hotchpotch of belongings. So as not to be separated amid the hordes, they had tied a dark blue cord around them all.

Reaching the Sangam in time for dawn, the legions of ordinary souls were stripping off their garments and wading into the water. Almond-eyed Assamese were bathing there along with thickset Punjabis from the north, and with swarthy Tamils from the Bay of Bengal. There were Hindus from the Himalayas and from Kolkata, from the Great Thar Desert and from the vast Indian diaspora that spans the world.

With the pink blush of first light touching the rippling surface, I pondered how little it all could have changed in centuries. And that's what made the Kumbh Mela so special to me — the sense that it was a circle of humanity linking us to our ancestors, to nature, and to our fellow men.

That night I took a taxi to the Allahabad railway station to take my train. The route was flooded and tens of thousands of pilgrims were wading through the overflowing sewers and conduits. With the traffic gridlocked for miles ahead, I abandoned the cab and joined everyone else on foot, my suitcase on my head.

Inside the station there were people everywhere. A great many were sprawled out on the platforms. Some were lying on carpets they had brought from home, others sharing their food with strangers, or in prayer. The atmosphere was convivial, a far cry from how it had been a few days before, when a footbridge had collapsed. In the resulting stampede thirty-six pilgrims had been trampled to death.

The dark blue sleeper train to Delhi rolled in, iron wheels grinding against the tracks. All of a sudden there was a frenzy of commotion as the pilgrims threw themselves at the train.

As I wondered how I would ever get aboard, I saw out of the corner of my eye a familiar face. This time it was smiling — it was the face of the wizened old woman from Bihar, her son's hand clasped tightly in her own.

THE LEGACY OF
ARAB SCIENCE

OCCIDENTAL SOCIETY TENDS to believe that the scientific and cultural bedrock upon which it sits was a product of the Classical world, most notably that of the Romans and the Greeks.

At our schools, teachers hold forth explaining Latin etymology, talking about the contributions of Euclid, Pythagoras, Plato and Aristotle. They remind us of the breakthroughs of these scholars and highlight how the knowledge amassed by Classical cultures has shaped our own world of learning.

But, in our obsession with the Romans and the Greeks, we blinker ourselves to the full picture. We forget how exactly the knowledge in our libraries, in our universities, and in our heads arrived there. And we forget how the breakthroughs of Classical culture were moulded to form the basis of modern Occidental civilization.

As usual with the transmission of knowledge, things weren't nearly as simple as we trick ourselves into believing. In reality, the knowledge of the Classical scholars passed through a matrix, a distinct system that honed it and gave it shape, rather like a swordsmith giving edge to a blade. As so often happens in human history, the lines of transmission are not straight, but zigzag.

Now, for the first time, historians are re-evaluating the way scientific thought developed, focusing on how one breakthrough fuelled another in both East and West. And, for the first time, the Occident is coming to terms with the extraordinary and pivotal contribution of Arab science — a contribution that allowed the world we recognize to be conjured into existence.

Without it, quite simply, most of the technology we know and take for granted wouldn't exist. The cell phone in my pocket wouldn't be able to communicate, and the laptop at which I'm typing wouldn't work. The hospital that kept me alive in the first week of life wouldn't have existed either. Nor would the technology that allowed me to hold this printed page. There wouldn't be panes of glass in the windows and, perhaps most of all, the technology that runs our computers and so shapes our lives today, simply wouldn't be there.

As someone who has one foot in the East and the other in the West, I find it extraordinary to remember the roll call of breakthroughs that can be attributed to Oriental society. More precisely, breakthroughs that came about between the ninth and thirteenth centuries CE, regarded as the golden age of Arab learning.

During this time, a wildfire of learning swept through the land, a realm that was fast expanding as the boundaries of the Islamic faith were pushed out in all directions. It was an era in which the first hospitals and lending libraries were constructed, and the first academic degrees presented. Mental patients were treated with music for the first time — more than a millennium before our idea of music therapy. And an endless catalogue of inventions was spawned from the learning centres which, in time, became the blueprint for our own Occidental universities.

The Arabs invented chemical apparatus, hydraulics systems and pharmaceuticals, astronomical tools, and even household soap. They wrote about the concepts of evolution, environmentalism, and pollution, outlined scientific method for the first time, as well as the idea of peer review. They shaped the building blocks of our own scientific culture and reworked all sorts of other things that are so critical to our world. It was through them that we received paper, the 'Indian' numbers, and the massive mathematical breakthrough of zero.

Arab contributions from the golden age span almost all the sciences. They can be found in mathematics and botany, in chemistry, psychology and philosophy, and in engineering, physics, agriculture and astronomy, in metallurgy, medicine and zoology.

The nucleus of almost all the technologies which govern our lives passed through Arab cultures — from the gears in our cars, to the watches on our wrists, to the satellites which bring us TV, and the know-how that makes the internet possible.

This lecture will give a snapshot of the role of Arab science, and consider the knock-on effect it had, allowing the Renaissance to take place, in turn enabling our world to be conjured.

The rise of Arab science really begins with the fall of the Roman Empire in 476 CE. At the rather traditional prep school I attended in England, they used to teach that centuries of darkness followed in the wake of the Roman collapse. Then, as though a lightning bolt from the heavens struck, came the European Renaissance. In between, so they taught me at any rate, there wasn't anything important to speak of — just a black hole of culture, a time that schoolboys learn (or used to learn) was called the 'Dark Ages'. No scholarship, no learning, no breakthroughs, just a desert of utter cultural and intellectual darkness.

Picture it: almost a thousand years when nothing really happened at all. And then, the Renaissance — the rebirth of learning — constructed solely on the bedrock of glorious Classical culture.

It sounds wonderfully romantic, but nothing could be farther from the truth.

To understand the present, we need to look carefully at how the Classics reached us. Because, like so often happens in human history, the lines of transmission aren't straight.

Please rest assured though — not for a minute am I going to pretend that the Arabs came up with everything from scratch. Far from it. And this is the key point: in the sciences, the Arabs took Classical work and refined it. They corrected the mathematics because they could, using the immensely powerful Indian numbers. It must have been like harnessing the power of a mainframe computer. But these numbers were just one arrow in their armoury of equipment. As we shall see, the Abbasids developed paper, and writing equipment, and they had a common language that was a *lingua franca* — all the way from Timbuktu in the west to Samarkand and beyond in the east.

Yet, given what we know, it seems remarkable to me that the Arab contribution — which was so profound — is often sidelined or completely forgotten altogether. And, very often, it was centuries ahead of its time.

All the while, the early Arab scholars committed their ideas to paper, allowing them to be circulated in the farthest reaches of the fledgling Islamic world. They wrote about the concepts of evolution and discussed what we would know as environmentalism, and classification (what we know as mineral, animal and vegetable), as well as coming up with clear scientific method.

Yet, for me, the most exciting thing of all was the way that the scientists were polymaths, working in half a dozen areas of study at the same time. This all-rounder approach allowed them to harness breakthroughs in one area, and apply cutting-edge know-how to other completely unrelated fields.

As I said, until very recently, Western science has tended to reject the Arab contribution, or even regard it as responsible for the destruction of Classical texts — rather than being their saviour.

But new scholarship in the West has shown that, by harnessing existing knowledge, and building upon it, the Arab contribution allowed the European Renaissance to take root. Yet perhaps worst of all is that the Arabs are themselves often ignorant of the immensely important role

they have played. They seem oblivious to the direct way
their communal scholarship has made the modern world
possible, almost as though they are toeing the Occidental
line.

So, how and where did it all begin — this amazing Arab
contribution? What was the spark?

It started in present day Kyrgyzstan, in Central Asia, on a
crisp July morning in the year 751 CE. The location was a
battlefield on the banks of the Talas River. And it was there
that the secret that made the rise of Arab learning possible,
passed from the Tang Chinese to the Abbasid Arabs. That
July morning was one of those pivotal moments in history, a
moment that's all too often forgotten.

By chance, the Arab conquerors — sweeping eastward
with Islam — won the battle. They weren't expected to do
so, and how they did is another story. The key point was
that they took prisoners, Chinese prisoners, who knew a
secret art — a technology that would change the world. It
was the art of papermaking. This secret was, until then,
known to a small elite fraternity, and was guarded day and
night. Indeed, well aware of the value of this technology, the
Arabs kept it secret from Europe for centuries. They built
papermaking factories in the intellectual nerve centres of
their new Islamic empire, at Baghdad, Damascus, Córdoba,
Fès and Samarkand.

For the first time, the Arabs could copy the Qur'an easily,
as well as other books — books devoted to the sciences.
Like a touchpaper being lit, it meant that knowledge could
be multiplied and passed up and down the pilgrimage

routes to centres of learning across the Islamic world. Paper quickly surpassed parchment and papyrus. It was far cheaper to make, and lightweight — so light that it could be conveyed by carrier pigeons. And it led directly to a vast library being built in Baghdad, to which I'll come in a moment.

And, as always with the golden age of Arab scholarship, the buzzword was 'innovation'. The Chinese had been making rough paper from mulberry bark since the second century BCE. It was best suited to the use of brushes rather than nibs. Never satisfied with existing technology, the Arabs refined their paper and used cotton pulp rather than tree bark. And they changed the equipment — using their newly designed waterwheels to power the paper mills, instead of human labour.

To understand the seismic change that was the golden age of Arab learning, you have to appreciate the time, the era of the Abbasids. After overthrowing the Umayyads, the second of the two great Islamic caliphates, the Abbasids ruled from 750 CE. They moved the capital from Damascus to Baghdad. In the ninth century it was a city of eight hundred thousand souls, second in population only to Constantinople. And it was ruled by one of the greatest leaders of all time, the Abbasid Caliph Harun ar-Rachid.

The city was a melting pot of humanity — people hailing from Europe, North Africa, Asia Minor and Central Asia. And this crucible of cultures was one that had never really been known before in human society, because under the new Islamic faith, all men were equal. And, most surprising of all, they could all communicate through Arabic, the *lingua franca* of Islam.

Harun, who tends to be remembered in the West above all else for his *Alf Layla wa Layla*, *A Thousand and One Nights*, set about accumulating books for a huge private library. He loved poetry, music and learning. Whenever he heard of erudite people, he invited them to his court. The idea of wisdom being rewarded for wisdom's sake spread, and scholars made their way from all corners of the growing Islamic world to Baghdad.

In March 809 CE, Harun ar-Rachid died, leaving the future of the caliphate hanging in deep uncertainty. He was succeeded by his son al-Amin, but he was killed four years later, which only made the situation more precarious. All that had been achieved so far was hanging in the balance. But then, thankfully, al-Amin's half-brother, al-Ma'mun, became caliph, and it is with him that our story really begins...

Like his father, Ma'mun was fascinated by learning, and was eager to know how the world and the universe worked. He built up the library founded by his father, and brought together scholars from every corner of the world, from every known religion, speaking every language. He dispatched messengers to bring forth to Baghdad every book, document, and sensible man in existence — and convey them back to his centre of learning, which became known as Bayt al Hikma, 'The House of Wisdom'.

What had started as the caliph's private library quickly became a translation centre, then a kind of think-tank, a repository of knowledge, with observatories and scientific centres attached. Hundreds of thinkers and scientists toiled away at the House of Wisdom, including some of the most important polymaths in human history, such as al-Kindi and al-Khwarizmi.

From the start, there must have been a sense that the House of Wisdom was different from anything that had come before, or at least since the Great Library at Alexandria.

The story goes that Caliph Ma'mun had a dream of white-haired Aristotle seated on a throne, a dream in which he was advised to begin a quest for wisdom through knowledge and reason. From the dream, Ma'mun interpreted that he should amass knowledge. Right away, he sent scholars to Byzantium to bring him academic texts, all of which were translated into Arabic.

Then, archives were brought from Alexandria, Damascus, Cairo and Antioch. A great number of the first books that arrived were in Greek, Latin and Persian as well. They were all translated into Arabic, along with others from Turkish, Syriac, Aramaic, Sanskrit and Chinese.

Over four centuries, scholars laboured away, translating collected knowledge and pushing forward the boundaries of science. The focus was very much on the cross-pollination of ideas and thinking in new ways. After all, until that moment, the emphasis had been on the reproduction by rote of accepted values and ideas.

Ma'mun led from the front. He funded the research and encouraged others to do so, and he also conferred formal prestige on scientists and intellectuals — lauding achievements with praise and financial remuneration.

In 832 CE, the year before he died, he is said to have travelled to Egypt, where he ordered his army to breach open the Great Pyramid of Cheops. It was still covered in white polished limestone casing stones. His army supposedly broke through the granite plug blocking access to the upper chambers. He was searching for treasure — gold perhaps, but it is more likely that the treasure he sought was knowledge.

Ma'mun was remarkable for his sheer innovation, as well as his ability to locate brilliant minds. He rewarded experimentation and anyone who tackled an old problem in a new way. He included plenty of non-Muslims at the House of Wisdom, and was ready to learn from them. It was a rare moment in history.

Through the House of Wisdom a model was created, one that was to be replicated again and again — such as at Dar al-Hikma in Cairo, a blueprint for something we would come to know as the university.

As I said, the great libraries that were established under the Abbasids came about owing to the existence of affordable paper, and growing literacy — a by-product of the fact that people were required to read the Qur'an. And these libraries were enormous, even by modern standards. The tenth-century Royal Library in Córdoba, for example, assembled under the patronage of Caliph al-Hakim II, boasted four hundred thousand books. The library's directory stretched to forty-four colossal ledgers. Caliph al-Hakim II sent scholars across the East to buy and have copied important books and, in so doing, he added to the expansion of knowledge.

The library at Cairo is said to have encompassed two million books, and the one at Tripoli had three million, before it was destroyed by Crusaders.

And, perhaps the greatest of all, that of the House of Wisdom itself in Baghdad, must have run into millions of volumes... before it was obliterated by the Mongol hordes.

A vast number of Classical texts, which no longer exist in their original Greek or Latin, were brought to the Renaissance through their Arabic translations. The Arabs not only translated entire treatises verbatim, but also reworked existing manuscripts. These new works drew on Greek and Roman classics, as well as Persian, Turkic and Indian sources.

And, just as there are Classical Greek and Latin texts that were saved by their Arabic translations, a great many Arabic texts — translated into Latin during the Renaissance — saved a number of key Arab works, which didn't survive in their original language.

But, whereas Latin was the language of scholarship, the clergy, and the elite throughout the Renaissance, Arabic was used by everyone during the golden age of Islam.

The Arab polymaths corrected a lot of Greek misconceptions, ideas passed on from one generation to the next, ideas that had been essentially set in stone. The Greek idea, for example, that light is emitted from the eye, allowing us to see. It wasn't until the tenth century CE that the Arab physicist al-Haytham (whose Latinized name is Alhazen) correctly stated that light bounces off an object in straight lines before striking the eye. He went on to develop the first camera obscura — which, centuries later, enabled photography.

Just like the Classical world before it, and the so-called 'Renaissance Men' after, the golden age of Islam was championed by polymaths, whose works easily rival those of Aristotle, Da Vinci or Newton.

The Arab polymaths arrived in the Renaissance under their Latinized names. As I said, al-Haytham was known as Alhazen. But there were many others, among them: Ibn Sina, who was known as Avicenna; Ibn Bajjah, known in the Occident as Avempace; Ibn Hayyan was Geber; and Ibn Rushd was Averroes. And perhaps the greatest of them all was Yakub al-Kindi, known in the West as Alkindus.

Using breakthroughs in one area of expertise, these polymaths pushed forward knowledge and understanding in another. Indeed, polymathy is a method that has almost been lost in the West, and is only now being rediscovered — so called 'interdisciplinary' study.

I recently heard a piece on the radio about Stanford University's new Bio-X Program. It brings together biologists, computer scientists, medical scientists and engineers, all of whom learn from each other's fields. The reporter presenting the piece was droning on about this amazing 'new' way of working — learning from each other. I rolled my eyes, and thought, 'Haven't you ever heard of the House of Wisdom, where scientists were learning from each other and solving huge problems more than a thousand years ago?'

The scientists and polymaths from the golden age worked on areas of science that are familiar to us all, disciplines that are still being studied in schools and universities today. Indeed, it was they who brought classification to the specific disciplines, while introducing clear practices that were absent in the Classical age.

For the first time there was clear scientific method — controlled experimentation and the idea of quantifying results. This new scientific method took off in a big way and was used across the board.

The first 'modern' medical experiment is known to have been carried out by al-Razi in the tenth century, when he was trying to decide where to build his hospital in Baghdad. He hung pieces of meat all over the city and observed where the meat decomposed the least quickly. It was there that he built the hospital. Pure genius if you think about it.

Another key piece of original Arab thinking was what we know as 'peer review'. It was first described by al-Rahwi, who was working in Damascus in the ninth century. In his *The Ethics of the Physician*, he states that the physician must always make duplicate notes of a patient's condition on every visit, so that when the patient has been discharged, or has died, one set of notes can be given to a local medical council, to ascertain whether satisfactory medical care has been provided. It marked the start of lawsuits for medical malpractice — more than a thousand years ago.

Medicine was at the core of science then, as it is today. During the golden age, the first hospitals were created, such as the one constructed by al-Razi. There were free public hospitals built across Baghdad and elsewhere — in Andalucía, North Africa, the Middle East, Central Asia and beyond. The main difference from the 'sleep temples' and asylums of the Classical era was that these hospitals were designed to treat and heal, rather than merely to isolate the infected and the sick. It was a revolutionary idea that caught on, and then spread to Europe, having been taken back there by the Christian Crusaders.

These first hospitals featured competency tests for doctors and surgeons, as well as grading for purity and strength of pharmaceuticals, and separate wards for people with similar contagious diseases. The first real autopsies were carried out, too, to work out why someone had died. And, in what was a completely cosmopolitan setting, the hospitals treated patients of different religions and cultures. The surgical staff comprised Christians and Jews as well as Muslims, and there were female doctors and nurses for the first time as well.

The rise in cheap paper, and literacy, meant that everything could be written down and passed to other cities along the pilgrimage routes, for others to learn from and master. This scholarship and know-how eventually reached Europe, where it was translated into Latin — although only the Latin-speaking elite could understand them.

Early pioneering works included the thirty-volume medical encyclopaedia, the *Kitab al-Tasrif* (The Book of Concessions), written by al-Zahrawi, which was first published in the year 1000 CE. It was used for centuries in both East and West. And there was Ibn Sina's *The Canon of Medicine* (written in about 1020 CE), still regarded as one of the most important medical textbooks of all time — it was used at the University of Montpellier's medical department as late as 1650 CE, and was relied on across China well into the nineteenth century.

Dozens of medical breakthroughs credited to the Renaissance, or to later scholars, had already been accurately described by the Arab polymaths of the golden age. Blood circulation, for instance, usually credited to the seventeenth-century English physician William Harvey, had been studied and described by Ibn al-Nafis in the thirteenth century.

The list of medical breakthroughs during this golden age is seemingly endless. The first inoculations against smallpox were carried out. There was the first description of micro-organisms, such as bacteria, centuries before the invention of the microscope. Dentistry, and pioneering work on dental fillings was done. Although, God help some of the patients. For example, Ibn Sina suggested that arsenic be boiled in oil and used to fill teeth!

Caesarean sections were performed with pain control. Antiseptics were developed and wounds were dressed with lint, sterilized with purified alcohol — itself an Arab discovery. Cataract surgery was performed, which used the first hollow metallic hypodermic needles and glass suction tubes, in about 1000 CE. Hundreds of other steel medical tools, such as scalpels, were pioneered — a result of sword-making breakthroughs and superior Damascene steel.

The first psychiatric hospital was built in Baghdad in 705 CE. Shortly after its construction, music therapy was pioneered. The area of study included the work of the tenth-century Persian music theorist al-Farabi, whose book *Meanings of the Intellect* discussed the effect of music on the soul. And, for the first time, specific diseases were isolated and studied, including diabetes, meningitis, and cancer, as well as rabies, smallpox, and forms of plague.

Reading accounts from the golden age of the Abbasids, you get a sense that a wildfire of learning was roaring east and west, north and south. New methods and ideas were being swapped face-to-face in teahouses, just as they were being exchanged by correspondence, linking scientists and polymaths all over the Islamic world and beyond. There was a sense of pure exhilaration, one that was mirrored later by the Renaissance, or by the Industrial Revolution and, more recently, by the birth of the internet.

New theories were hammered out and challenged — the most brilliant minds of the day working at fever pitch in the fledgling universities founded across the Islamic world. The theory of evolution, for example, was widespread by the twelfth century. One of the pioneers of such thinking was al-Jahiz. Working in ninth-century Baghdad, he wrote about the effect of the environment on an animal, and the animal's chances of survival based on the environment. He came up with something he termed 'the struggle for existence', a forerunner of Darwin's 'natural selection'.

During the golden age, the great thirst of scholarship was to understand the world around us, how it all worked, and how it was interrelated. As always, one question led to another, as did one answer to the next. Understandings relating to our environment and the natural world allowed for breakthroughs in agriculture. These included developing practices for pollination, pesticides, irrigation, grafting, crop rotation and soil preparation, as well as the classification of plants. Works, such as those by the thirteenth-century Andalucían botanist al-Baitar, were used in Europe for centuries to come. His masterwork listed fourteen hundred plants (three hundred of which he discovered himself). Translated into Latin, it was kept in print until 1758, and used until the start of the nineteenth century. And, as ever, the knock-on effects continued. Breakthroughs in water technology and hydraulics, for example, meant that areas that had been barren could be irrigated, and man could control his environment in ways that had never been possible before.

And, as the scientists began to understand their world from the inside out, they developed new fields of study. Modern chemistry may owe more to Arab science than any other area. Its very name is, of course, derived from *al-kimiya*, the Arab word for alchemy.

Although alchemy was very important, and had come to the Arabs from both India and the Roman Empire, we now understand increasingly how many Abbasid scientists rejected the belief in transmuting base metals into gold.

Arab breakthroughs in chemistry were plentiful, and were aided by new scientific practices, as we have seen. They included the isolation of new chemicals and an array of technical processes.

Distillation equipment, for instance, was developed — including alembic apparatus, stills and retorts — allowing for alcohol to be distilled for the first time. The product was used for perfume and in medical sterilization, rather than for drinking.

Kerosene, which was used in lamps, was distilled from crude oil by al-Razi in ninth-century Baghdad. He described the process in his *Kitab al-Asrar* (Book of Secrets). Other petroleum products were known and used. The streets of Baghdad, for instance, were paved with tar in the eighth century. And Arab scientists first distilled crude oil to create a form of what we know as petrol.

Other processes were developed and refined, including crystallization, filtration, and steam distillation. Strong acids were created for the first time, such as nitric, hydrochloric, and sulphuric acid. Amazingly, the Greeks and Romans had only known and used vinegar. At the same time, other elements were discovered, such as arsenic and antimony, and the chemical elements were clearly divided into categories and studied.

The result was a range of products which made ordinary life much better. Soap, for instance, was manufactured for the first time; and even glue was made... from cheese — a secret recipe described in ibn Hayyan's *The Book of the Hidden Pearl*.

Cosmetics were developed as well, including those by the fabulous-sounding Ziryab, 'The Blackbird' — a former Persian slave, who is also credited with inventing toothpaste. The idea caught on like nothing else. He went on to open a beauty parlour in Andalucían Spain and, supposedly, pioneered underarm deodorants and the chemical removal of unwanted body hair for women.

studied the Milky Way with a telescope, that he discovered it was composed of a huge number of faint stars.

As a byproduct, Arab astronomy developed numerous pieces of equipment for measuring angles and so forth — such as quadrants and, importantly, astrolabes. These were used for measuring the distance of celestial bodies above the horizon, as well as in determining latitude.

And it was astronomy that led indirectly to breakthroughs in yet another area — geography. The lightning speed with which Islam had spread by the eighth century — from Iberia to modern Afghanistan — paved the way for a complete reappraisal of geography. New information was flooding into research centres in Baghdad, Cairo, Damascus, Córdoba and elsewhere, and new technology (such as quadrants and astrolabes) was used to create ever-more accurate maps.

Perhaps the greatest map of all was al-Idrisi's twelfth-century atlas, prepared for the Norman King Roger II of Sicily in 1154 CE. It incorporated Africa, Europe, Asia Minor, India and the known world, stretching eastward to the Far East. The first atlas of its kind ever produced, it took eighteen years to complete.

As astronomy developed, so did mathematics and geometry. The great Arab polymaths changed the world in which we live through their mastery of mathematics.

Without doubt the most important breakthrough was the language of mathematics: the introduction of

'Arabic' numerals from India, and the use for the first time of a decimal point. The Arab golden age was a time of conduits — none more striking than that which linked the Classical world with that of the Renaissance.

Introducing zero to mainstream mathematics was the other astonishing breakthrough — the idea of representing 'nothing' with a symbol. It was such an inspired concept that we can even now hardly grasp its importance.

In the ninth century, Persian polymath al-Khwarizmi gave us algorithms, which form the basis of most computer programming... indeed our word 'algorithm' is derived from his name. Al-Khwarizmi is credited with writing the first book on algebra as well. Its title was *The Compendious Book on Calculation by Completion and Balancing* and it was published in about 820 CE.

Arab mathematics honed the work of the Greeks and the Romans, as well as that of South Asia. And this work was channelled directly into Europe through Islamic Spain and, with time, was made available to the great minds of the Renaissance.

The availability of a rock-solid mathematical framework allowed the offshoots to proliferate. And the contributions of some breakthroughs are only now being discovered. Little more than twenty years ago, a scholar roving through the Ottoman archives in Istanbul happened upon a manuscript which, it seems, had lain dormant for more than a thousand years. Entitled *On Deciphering Cryptographic Messages*, the work was none other than al-Kindi's treatise on cryptanalysis: the first paper ever to describe what was — until quite recently — the backbone of all code-breaking.

The golden age was a time of wonder and a time of excellence — so many fine minds coming together, reaching new intellectual frontiers. And, for all the number-crunching and dry scholarship, there were dazzling outgrowths.

My favourite area of all is that of the inventions.

I've mentioned a few already — devices in medicine, chemistry and astronomy. But there are whole other areas in which the Arabs excelled.

Arab engineers learned from the Romans, Greeks, and from their own scientists, arriving at creations that demonstrated their astonishing ingenuity. Some extended life and improved living conditions, while others were more whimsical, as we shall see.

Engineers were hugely important during the Abbasid Caliphate. When the tenth-century Persian physicist and polymath Ibn al-Haytham (Alhazen) reached Cairo, the caliph himself went to the gates to great him. He had been invited to regulate the flooding on the Nile. It soon dawned on him that he couldn't solve the problem. The only way to save his neck was to feign madness and live for years under house arrest, biding his time until the caliph's own death.

Windmills were a key piece of technology, and one that has come to the fore again, as we harness the winds. They were first described by Persian geographer Estakhri in the ninth century. Being used to grind corn and draw up water, they reached Europe through Islamic Spain.

The first hydro-powered water supply system — driven by gears — was developed by al-Jazari in Damascus to supply water to the city's mosques and hospitals. Fès had a similar system which worked until relatively recently, the remnants clearly visible in the medina, on Talaa Kebira.

As I have said, water was used to power paper mills and all sorts of other ingenious devices. Water wheels, or 'norias' as they are known, were developed for feeding water into aqueducts. The newly invented crankshaft was added, and the technology was constantly refined.

In addition to crankshafts, Arab engineers devised flywheels, chain pumps, gearing systems, suction pumps, and automata.

The greatest and most celebrated engineer of the era was without doubt al-Jazari, whose technical breakthroughs in the twelfth century can still be found all around us today. His masterwork was *The Book of Knowledge of Ingenious Mechanical Devices*. He developed the first automatic gates, run on water power, as well as accurate water clocks, and the flush mechanism still used in toilets. But it was his work with humanoid automata that gained him the most attention. His full-sized models of people would serve chilled drinks and play music, wooing his wealthy patrons, and so ensuring that funding for his real work didn't dry up.

Al-Jazari's most brilliant yet fanciful device was a vast elephant clock, powered by water, and featuring a dragon, a phoenix, and a golden howdah upon which a prince was seated. Shortly after this *pièce de résistance* of curious engineering was created, the golden age of the Abbasids came to an abrupt end.

It was as if the 'stop' button was pressed on a culture that had achieved so much in such a remarkably short span of time. The reason for this cessation of know-how?

The Mongol invasion.

In 1257, the grandson of Genghis Khan, Hulagu Khan, set out for Baghdad with a vast army. The caliph refused to surrender and enraged the Mongol leader with threats. Worse still, he hadn't strengthened the city walls or prepared for a siege. As a result, victory was swift, the siege lasting less than two weeks. The caliph capitulated on February 10th 1258.

Seven days and nights followed of looting, rape, pillage, and utter destruction. Baghdad was sacked and burned to the ground. The waters of the Tigris were said to have run black with ink for weeks when the House of Wisdom's and other libraries were hurled into the river.

The caliph was, it was said, rolled up in a carpet before the Mongols rode their horses up and down over him. So great was the stench of death and decay that Hulagu had to move his camp upwind of the city. As for Baghdad, the great capital of learning, it lay ruined for centuries — its population, wealth, and treasure houses of knowledge decimated.

Rather than end on the thought of Mongolian slaughter, I'd like to conclude with a glimmer of hope.

In the centuries since the golden age of the Abbasids, some good scholarship has taken place in translating and studying the surviving works from Bayt al Hikma, the House of Wisdom. As I have described, the availability of affordable paper — coupled with literacy and the pilgrimage routes — allowed scholars to send copies of their works to libraries thousands of miles away. The result was that a great number of key texts survived the Mongol horde. Indeed, there are far more Arabic manuscripts in existence from medieval Islam than from the Roman and Greek world.

And the glimmer of hope: thousands of Arabic texts are still untranslated, lying dormant in archives and libraries across the West and the East.

So, the next time you reach for your mobile phone, or write an email on your laptop, or use Google, please spare a thought for the golden age of the Abbasids.

After all, without them, I doubt that many of us would be here today.

A REQUEST

If you enjoyed this book, please review it on your favourite online retailer or review website.

Reviews are an author's best friend.

To stay in touch with Tahir Shah, and to hear about his upcoming releases before anyone else, please sign up for his mailing list:

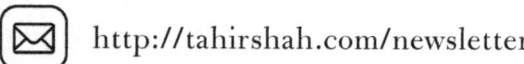 http://tahirshah.com/newsletter

And to follow him on social media, please go to any of the following links:

http://www.twitter.com/humanstew

@tahirshah999

http://www.facebook.com/TahirShahAuthor

http://www.youtube.com/user/tahirshah999

http://www.pinterest.com/tahirshah

https://www.goodreads.com/tahirshahauthor

http://www.tahirshah.com